I Met H
At The Well

by
Katherine Goody

To Rosemary
God bless you
Katherine x

With love and thanks to, my husband Roger,
for all his encouragement and support.
And to Pastors Robert & Virginia Maasbach,
and The Life Church, Folkestone, Kent,
for their teaching and spiritual guidance.

It is God to whom and with whom we travel, and while He
is the end of our journey,
He is also at every stopping place. - Elisabeth Elliot

I MET HIM AT THE WELL

I met him at the well that day,
The man with the world in his eyes.
He looked into my heart and knew me by name,
Saw through my sadness, sorrow and pain.
Everything about me he understood,
Oh how I wondered, how was it he could.

I met him at the well that day,
The man with the world in his eyes.
I bowed low my head as he asked for a drink,
I could not look up fearful of what he would think.
Come unto me, he said, drink from my cup
The water I offer will never dry up.

I met him at the well that day,
The man with the world in his eyes.
The cup that he offered was full of joy, peace and love
I knew he was sent from my father above.
Living water to satisfy day after day
He is the truth, the life and the way.

I met him at the well that day,
The man with the world in his eyes.
I lay down my life and took hold of his hand
He leads me on and with him I will stand.
Forgiven and loved by my saviour and friend
With my Jesus forever unto the end.

by Katherine Goody.

Foreword

Being a Christian is a life's work, it cannot be attained over night by simply believing. Becoming a Christian happens instantly when we acknowledge Jesus as the Son of God and our Lord and Saviour, but being a Christian is something we walk out daily, hand in hand with Jesus, over the mountains and through the valleys, trusting Him to keep us and lead us. As we travel the road of life we may not feel we have come very far, achieved very much, or we may feel that Jesus has left us to struggle alone. But it is in the looking back we see just how far the Lord has brought us, changed us and how much we have overcome and accomplished with Him by our side. The further down the road I get the more amazed I am at just how much the Lord has done in my life, and I am excited at how much yet He is going to do. In writing this book it is my desire to bring those at the crossroads to make the decision to follow Him and to encourage others to carry on and not give up in their walk with Christ. In the Bible in the book of Revelation it says in Chapter 12 v.11, that they overcame by the blood of the lamb and the word of their testimony. These are the words of my testimony. I pray that the Lord will bless you as you read.

The following versions of the Bible have been used in this work.

NIV New International Version

NKJV New King James Version. The Spirit filled life Bible .

Contents

Chapter 1

In the beginning was the Word

Born and raised in Essex my childhood was a happy one. I grew into a happy confident young woman and was popular with my peers and enjoyed life. As a child I had been encouraged to attend Sunday school, not because my parents were church goers but because it was what you did in the 50's. Sunday afternoon the kiddies went off to church and Mum and Dad put their feet up and had a quiet afternoon. I found it fun, I enjoyed playing with my friends but it didn't mean any more to me than just nice stories It wasn't until I was thirty and trying to make sense of my life following a divorce that I found Jesus. Or should I say He found me.

I had grown up with a group of friends and gradually we all paired up and got married. We were just twenty and I thought I knew him well, he was fun loving, great company, attentive, got on well with my family, an all round nice guy. Or so I thought. After the wedding he began to change choosing to spend time with others rather than me. Finding fault in everything I did, belittling me in front of family and friends and telling me I was fat and ugly. He didn't want to be with me but he didn't want me to go out either, I was confused. If we went out together he would push me on to someone else so he could go off and do what he wanted. Gradually the happy, confident person I used to be was gone. I couldn't understand what I had done to make him change. I had hoped that when we had our children things would improve. For a while our relationship was better but then he changed again. Now blaming them for everything, staying out only coming home to change his clothes or go to bed. I thought I must be me doing something wrong and I tried to become the person he seemed to want, but that didn't work either. The man I married had become a bully. Eventually I begun not to want him to come home, life was quiet and peaceful without him . I knew he was seeing other women, but by this time I really didn't care and thought they were welcome to him. We both begun living separate lives putting on a mask pretending all was well. During this time I met someone else. My knight in shinning armour. He was loving, kind, considerate and made me feel beautiful again, but he was married. We had an affair and it was wonderful but eventually we began to want more. I was happy but I felt so guilty, I was taking someone else's husband. My marriage finally ended and we divorced. From then on I was in constant turmoil not knowing what to do. I so wanted to be with my new man but I knew it was wrong. My conscience eventually got the better of me and I ended the affair. It broke my heart and I was lost, I didn't know where to turn. I couldn't talk to family or friends as I felt so ashamed. So I threw myself in to making new friends trying to find the attention I sort in others, in other men. I was on a downward spiral and couldn't get off and I began to wonder what the point to it all was.

The only good thing I had left in my life was my two dear children and it was through a friendly neighbour inviting me to a Mother and Toddler group that my life started to change. The people were so kind and friendly, I felt comfortable and able to be myself without fear of judgement or accusation. It was part of the local Baptist Church and they suggested I might like to take the children to Sunday school. Initially I would just take the children to Sunday school and go home for a bit of peace and quiet but one day I decided to stay for the Church service and see what it was all about. That day changed my life. Jesus came into my heart and I drank from the well that will never run dry. He spoke to me through the darkness, reached in and took hold of me and changed my life as nothing or no one else could.

That Sunday the Pastors sermon was from the book of John Chapter 4: verses 7 – 26. Jesus talks with a Samaritan Woman.

7. A Samaritan woman came to draw water; Jesus said to her, "Will you give me a drink?" 8. (His disciples had gone into the town to by food) 9. The Samaritan woman said to him, "You are a Jew and I am a Samaritan woman. How can you ask me for a drink?" (for Jews do not associate with Samaritans). 10. Jesus answered her, "If you knew the gift of God and who it is that asks you for a drink, you would have asked him and he would have given you living water." 11. "Sir", the woman said, "you have nothing to draw with and the well is deep. Where can you get this living water?

12. Are you greater than our father Jacob, who gave us the well and drank from it himself, as did also his sons and his flocks and herds?" 13. Jesus answered, "Everyone who drinks this water will thirst again, 14. but whoever drinks the water I give him will never thirst. Indeed, the water I give him will become in him a spring of water welling up to eternal life." 15. The woman said to Him, "Sir, give me this water so that I won't get thirsty and have to keep coming here to draw water."

16. He told her, "Go, call your husband and come back." 17. "I have no husband," she replied. Jesus said to her, "You are right when you say you have no husband. 18. The fact is, you have had five husbands, and the man you now have is not your husband. What you have just said is quite true."

19. "Sir," the woman said, "I can see that you are a prophet. 20. Our fathers worshipped on this mountain, but you Jews claim that the place where we must worship is in Jerusalem." 21. Jesus, declared, "Believe me, woman, a time is coming, when you will worship the Father neither on this mountain nor in Jerusalem. 22. You Samaritans worship what you do not know; we worship what we do know, for salvation is from the Jews. 23. Yet a time is coming and has now come when the true worshippers will worship the Father in Spirit and Truth, for they are the kind of worshippers the Father seeks. 24. God is spirit, and his worshippers must worship in spirit and truth." 25. The woman said, "I know that the Messiah (called Christ) is coming. When he comes, he will explain everything 26. Then Jesus declared, "I who speak to you am he."

I had heard about Jesus before but that day I met Him.

Chapter 2

The Meeting at the Well

Let's look at Jesus words in the Book of John. Chapter 4 again.

v.7 A Samaritan woman came to draw water, Jesus said to her, "Will you give me a drink?"

Like the Samaritan woman Jesus caught my attention, it was as though I was actually with Him at the well. I felt I was the only one in Church and He was talking to me.

v.9 The Samaritan woman said to him, "You are a Jew and I am a Samaritan, how can you ask me for a drink?" (Jews did not associate with Samaritans.)

Like the Samaritan woman I was questioning why He was talking to me. He was Jesus, Gods Son, and me, well I was nothing . A sinner, my life was a mess, I wasn't worthy to kiss the soles of His feet let alone talk to Him. And yet He was talking to me!

v. 14,15 "Whoever drinks the water that I give him will never thirst. Indeed the water I give will become in him a spring of water welling up to eternal life." The woman said to Him, " Sir, give me this water so that I won't get thirsty and have to keep coming here to draw water."

Jesus was inviting me to come to Him, to drink from the well that will never run dry. I did not understand, yet each week I was drawn to church, drawn to the well. I was searching for an answer to my life.

v. 16-18. Jesus said to her, "Go call your husband and come back." "I have no husband," she replied. "You are right when you say you have no husband. The fact is, you have had five husbands and the man you now have is not your husband", Jesus answered.

Jesus knew all about me and yet, He still wanted to know me.

That morning in Church I felt that Jesus was talking to me, not the Pastor, but Jesus. Something inside me came alive and I knew that I had to drink from the cup He was offering me, I knew that with Jesus by my side everything would be alright. I saw in Him love and forgiveness and a hope for tomorrow. He wanted to be my Lord and Saviour. All this was unconditional, a gift. He wanted to be my friend, He promised help and strength. I knew He was the answer to my problems.

As I sat there with tears streaming down my face, the Pastor gave an alter call and asked for people who wanted to receive Jesus to come to the front of the Church. I wanted to go but I could not move, it was as though I was having a tug of war inside me. I saw others go forward, I saw the Pastor praying with them but yet I could not move. I don't know how long I sat there frozen to my seat but the next thing I remember is someone putting their hand on my shoulder. As I turned the Pastor looked into my eyes and asked if I would like to receive Jesus. My tears turned to sobs, I cried and cried like I would never stop. All my hurts and pains pouring from my soul. Eventually when my cries had subsided the Pastor prayed with me and I received Jesus as my Lord and Saviour.

I have never known such peace or felt such love and acceptance, I wanted to stay in that place forever.

Chapter 3

Jesus is the answer

I am sure many of you can relate to my story. Relate to feelings of failure, of rejection, of worthlessness, depression, fear and despair, not knowing what to do next and feeling there is no hope for tomorrow.

But we do have a hope. 1 Peter 1:3 In His great mercy He has given us new birth into a living hope through the resurrection of Jesus Christ from the dead and into an inheritance that can never perish, spoil or fade.

We are worth something. Deuteronomy 26:18 The Lord has declared this day that you are His people, His treasured possession.

We have a Saviour who is for us and not against us. Romans 8:31 If God is for us, who can be against us.

God loves us so much that He sent His only son Jesus as a living sacrifice for our sins and to bring us life in abundance today and eternal life tomorrow. John 3:16 For God so loved the world He gave His only son that whosoever believes in Him shall have eternal life.

Whose gift of love is freely given. Ephesians 2:4 Because of His great love for us, God, who is rich in mercy, made us alive with Christ even when we were dead in transgressions. It is by grace we have been saved.

There is no fear in love. But perfect love drives out all fear. 1 John 4:18

In whom we are more than conquerors over depression and despair. Romans 8:37 In all things we are more than conquerors through Him who loved us.

In whom there is no condemnation. Romans 8:1 Therefore there is now no condemnation for those who are in Christ Jesus.

Who removes our sins from us. Psalm 103:12 As far as the east is from the west, so far has He removed our transgressions from us.

Who washes us whiter than snow. Isaiah 1:18 Though your sins are like scarlet, they shall be as white as snow.

Who gave us Jesus to carry our burdens. Jesus says in Matthew 11:28,29 , "Come to me all of you who are weary and burdened and I will give you rest. Take my yoke upon you and learn from me, for I am gentle and humble in heart and you will find rest for your souls. For my yoke is easy and my burden light.

Jesus is sufficient for all our needs, there is nothing that He cannot do for us. Corinthians 12:9 My grace is sufficient for you.

You may have heard of Jesus before, but today He wants to meet you.

As I asked Jesus into my life so you can too. He can begin that process of bestowing on you a crown of beauty instead of ashes, giving you the oil of gladness instead of mourning and a garment of praise instead of a spirit of despair. All you have to do is ask and He will come in and make His home with you.

Invite Him into your heart today and receive new life!!

Let us pray - Father I come to you. I know I have sinned in thought and word and deed and I have not lived my life as you have desired. In your mercy please forgive me. I thank you for your son Jesus who died on the cross as a living sacrifice to wash away my sins and bring me life. Eternal life and life in abundance today. I choose to turn my back on the life I have lived without you and I invite Jesus into my heart as my Lord and Saviour. I thank you that from this moment, I am yours and you are mine.

Amen.

Chapter 4

Repent and be Baptised

Acts 2: 38 Repent and be baptised, every one of you, in the name of Jesus Christ for the forgiveness of your sins.

I was baptised on the 16th November, 1986. Before my unsaved family and friends I declared Jesus to be my Lord and Saviour. I gladly laid down my old life and took hold of my new life in Christ. I vowed from that moment to follow Jesus all my days.

After Jesus was baptised by John the Baptist He went into the desert for forty days and forty nights and was tempted by the devil. You can read about this in the book of Matthew Chapters 3 and 4. We too, become prey to the devil's deceptions and lies.

Jesus came into my life and began His work in me. He took my hand and walked with me through the good and the bad times gently leading me to the place I am in today. However, I can remember how I used to always feel a failure, as no matter how much I tried to change and do the right thing I was forever getting it wrong.

Romans 7:15 I do not understand what I do. For what I want to do I do not do, but what I hate I do.

God shows us through His word in the Bible that we are in very good company. There are many cases of mighty men and women of God who failed.

One example is King David who although called and anointed of God was led into temptation through Bathsheba.

'And from the roof he saw a woman bathing and the woman was very beautiful to behold.'
Samuel 11:2

David's lustful gaze led to lustful thoughts and this resulted in him taking Bathsheba as his own. One sin led to another and to cover himself he had Bathsheba's husband Uriah killed.

2 Samuel 11:15 "Set Uriah in the forefront of the hottest battle and retreat from him that he may be struck down and die."

David acknowledges that it was against God only that he had sinned. He repented for having violated God himself, His person and His nature. He was a broken man before God; he humbled himself completely at God's mercy.

Psalm 51: 4 Against You, You only have I sinned.

Although David's heart was crushed by his shame and sorrow over sin, he knew the great breadth of God's mercy. He knew that His God would have mercy upon him because of His loving-kindness. When we look at David and the extent of his sin and the extent of God's forgiveness we can draw such encouragement for our own lives. Not only did God forgive David but He restored and blessed him more than before. He never said, that's it I am not going to use you, you've failed, He turned David's failures into His victories. God can do the same for us, and how much more through the blood of Jesus.

Chapter 5

What I want to do I do not do, and what I hate I do. (Romans 7:15)

As a new Christian I failed bitterly. I committed adultery, continuing my relationship with the married man I had known before I came a Christian. When I found myself pregnant with his baby, my sin became public.

Before I go any further, I would like to state, that there has never been a moment now or then when I considered the baby I was carrying to be a mistake or accident. He has been loved and wanted from the moment of conception. Neither does God make mistakes, He knows the plans and purposes He has for each one of us. He has the days of our life written in His book. Our son Matthew today is a mighty man of God. Completely and utterly sold out to serve Christ. Full of the Holy Spirit, an anointed and gifted musician. He is no failure, mistake or accident.

Psalm 139 v. 13-16
For you O lord created my inmost being, you knit me together in my mother's womb. I praise you because I am fearfully and wonderfully made, your works are wonderful, I know that full well. My frame was not hidden from you when I was made in the secret place. When I was woven together in the depths of the earth, your eyes saw my unformed body. All the days ordained for me were written in your book before one of them came to be.

The Lord turns all things together for good. Romans 8:28 All things God works for the good of those who love Him. He uses every situation for His glory when we give them to Him, standing firm in our faith. So often as I look back over my life I see difficult times,

11

sad times, things that have gone wrong and I see how the Lord has turned them around and used them for His Glory. Good comes from them and we are blessed. You only need to read the book of Job to understand this principle completely.

The months leading up to my son's birth were hard and although I continued to attend church it became increasingly difficult. I found it hard to accept people's reactions. Whispers behind closed door, the pious looks and words of sympathy. Those who had been friends no longer spoke to me and would not sit next to me in church. My children were teased and taunted by their peers in Sunday school. Bit by bit I began to feel rejected and alone once more. All my old failings came back to haunt me and I began to wonder if Jesus had rejected me too.

Although my partner Roger wasn't a Christian at this time it was he who encouraged me to hold on to my faith. To put my worries and fears in God's hands. As I was drawn to my knees and to Jesus and His word, He showed me that He doesn't give up on us and that His mercies are new every morning.

Lamentations 3:23 Because of the Lord's great love we are not consumed, for His compassions never fail. They are new every morning, great is your faithfulness.

Once we have made that step in baptism and placed our hand in His He will never let us go.

Isaiah 43: 1-2 I have called you by our name when you pass through the waters I will be with you. And through the rivers; they shall not overflow you.

Hebrews 13:5 Never will I leave you; never will I forsake you.

No matter what others said I could not believe the Jesus I knew would turn me away. When a situation arose I would ask myself, "What would Jesus do if He were here", and the answer would always be, love me. I drew strength from His love and His promises in the Bible. I was amazed at how the scriptures were opened up to me, how they spoke directly in to my life.

However badly we mess up God is always there ready to forgive and welcome us back when we turn to him and repent. I prayed for forgiveness, I knew what I had done was wrong and I knew that continuing to live with the baby's father was wrong, but when the church told me I could no longer attend church unless I lived without him, I didn't know what to do. We wanted to get married but as he was still awaiting his divorce settlement it was not possible. I knew I could not live without his help and support with our son, everyone else had turned from me, I couldn't face loosing him too. So I left the church.

Quote Mother Theresa – 'Nowhere in the gospel has Christ uttered an expression of rejection. Rather, we always find an invitation: Come to me.'

Chapter 6

Go now and leave your life of sin

John 8 v. 4 – 11

The teachers of the law and the Pharisees brought in a woman caught in adultery. They made her stand before the group and said to Jesus. "Teacher, this woman was caught in the act of adultery. In the Law Moses commanded us to stone such women. Now what do you say?" They were using this question as a trap in order to have a basis for accusing him. But Jesus bent down and started to write on the ground with his finger. When they kept on questioning him, he straightened up and said to them, "If any one of you is without sin, let him be the first to throw a stone at her". Again he stooped down and wrote on the ground. At this, those who heard began to go away one at a time, the older ones first, until only Jesus was left, with the woman still standing there. Jesus straightened up and asked her. "Woman, where are they? Has no one condemned you " No-one sir", she said. "Then neither do I condemn you", Jesus declared. "Go now and leave you life of sin".

When the woman was caught in adultery and was about to be stoned, Jesus forgave her and didn't judge her but told her to go and leave her life of sin. I believed God had forgiven me and didn't judge me but I couldn't understand why the church rejected me. God didn't judge me, He forgave me, He didn't reject me so why should they.

I have spent many years struggling with this, blaming myself, blaming others, and blaming God. But we fight not against flesh and blood but against principalities and powers of darkness. The fight is in the spirit. The devil wants to keep us down. Not only does he tempt us and lie to us and lead us astray he wants to keep us there, in our place of failure and confusion. I attended other Churches but I could not find peace or acceptance. I felt that if people found out what I was like they would ask me to leave their Church too. I prayed and ask the Lord to help me break this stronghold that was keeping me from God's plan and purpose for my life and from declaring what He had done for me.

Praise the Lord, that when we call upon His name He answers us. He hears our cries and knows exactly what we need even before it is on our lips.

The Lord led me to a church where I began to feel loved and accepted and through the preaching and the teaching the scriptures were opened up to me. He even gave me the courage to share my story with the Pastor and through sharing and praying together I found the peace that I sort.

2 Corinthians 7.10 Godly sorrow brings repentance that leads to salvation and leaves no regret, but worldly sorrow brings death.

If we hold on to our failures of the past they affect our future. We need to confess our sins to one another. Repent take responsibility for our actions. Say yes, I messed up but I have a Saviour who died on the cross to take my sins away, wash me whiter than snow and sit me at the right hand of the Father. We have a way out. God has provided a way out for us when we mess up. He disciplines us when we fail as a natural Father disciplines his child because he loves them. But if in humility we turn to Him in true repentance He will wash us in the blood of Jesus and remove even the thought of our sin from our minds. The devil will no longer have a hold over us, he will no longer be able to accuse us or others and his power over the situation will be broken. I have learnt that true repentance means to turn completely from our sin and sin no more, and with God's help we can achieve this and find freedom that breaks those chains that bind. As Jesus said to the woman caught in adultery, "Go now and leave your life of sin."

If we ignore such a great salvation we are responsible for crucifying Jesus again and again. Jesus died once and for all to take away the sin of the world, should we expect him to do it again just for us because we cannot forgive or accept forgiveness. Often we can feel that if we let go of our hurts or forgive someone, then they are getting away with it. When in effect it is ourselves we are hurting in separating ourselves from God.

It was for freedom that Jesus has set us free. Let us live in that freedom not bound continually by our sin or failings.

Just think if King David had held on to his failures there would have been no Jesus. If Peter had held on to his failures many people would not have heard about Jesus. If we hold on to our failures we stop what God wants to work through us. If I had held on to my failures I would not be able today to testify of what the Lord had done in my life, encourage others and lead them to Jesus.

Ephesians 2:4 But because of His great love for us, God who is rich in mercy, makes us alive with Christ even when we were dead in transgressions – it is by grace you have been saved, not by works, so that no one can boast.

We cannot earn our salvation we can only work it out with the help of the Holy Spirit.

John 14:v16 Jesus said, "I will ask the Father, and he will give you another Counsellor to be with you for ever – the Spirit of truth. v.26 The Counsellor, the Holy Spirit, whom the Father will send in my name will teach you all things and will remind you of everything I have said to you.

God didn't leave us alone to struggle with our failings, He knew we could never make it on our own, but He gave us the Holy Spirit to help us in our weakness.

Romans 8:15 For you did not receive a spirit that makes you a slave again to fear, but you received the Spirit of sonship. And by him we cry, "Abba Father ".

Romans 8:26 In the same way, the Spirit helps us in our weakness. We do not know what we ought to pray for, but the Spirit himself intercedes for us with groans that words cannot express.

Our Salvation is a process. Daily we work out our salvation by God's grace and with the help of the Holy Spirit. We never cease to learn and grow. Just remember what Jesus said to us at the well. "Everyone that drinks the water that I give him will never thirst". Whenever we feel a failure, when we face that mountain in our life, go back to Jesus, to the well, let him fill you anew, refresh you and revive you.

'As sure as God allows his children in the furnace, He will be in the furnace with them.'

Chapter 7

In all things we are more than conquerors (Romans 8:37)

With the help of the Holy Spirit Roger and I overcame the problems and were married eighteen months after our sons birth. Although Roger was not then a Christian we were married in church, in the sight of God. Although this is a very controversial subject and I know many Christians will not agree with some of my philosophy here. I truly believe that it has been because we were married in God's sight that His hand has been upon us as a couple and a family. Looking after us all and working out His plans and purpose for our lives. In an ideal world it is far better for a Christian to marry another Christian. You both have the same goal, the same beliefs you are both going in the same direction. But like many others today I found myself in a less than ideal situation and as we have said before God works all things together for good for those who love him.

My mission field was then as it still is today for my unsaved family. I will never cease praying for their salvation and I have full confidence in my God to do what He has promised. He has given me many words concerning this from the Bible.

God's promises for my family

Joshua 24:15 As for me and my household we will serve the Lord.

Isaiah 49:18 Lift up your eyes and look around; all your sons gather and come to you. As surely as I live, declares the Lord, you will wear them all as ornaments, you will put them on, like a bride.

Isaiah 49: 25 I will contend with those who contend with you, and your children I will save.

Isaiah 54:11-13 I will build you with stones of turquoise, your foundations with sapphires. I will make your battlement of rubies, your gates of sparkling jewels, and all your walls of precious stones. All your sons will be taught by the Lord, and great will be your children's peace.

Isaiah 58: 11-13 The Lord will guide you always; he will satisfy your needs in a sun-scorched land and will strengthen your frame. You will be like a well-watered garden, like a spring whose waters never fail. Your people will rebuild the ancient ruins and will raise up the age-old foundations; you will be called, Repairer of Broken Walls, Restorer of Streets with Dwellings.

Isaiah 59:21 As for me, this is my covenant with them says the Lord. My Spirit, who is on you, and my words that I have put in your mouth, will not depart from your mouth, or from the mouths of your children, or from the mouths of their descendants from this time on and forever, says the Lord.

Even when things look impossible we must stay in faith and believe that what God has said He will do.

Psalm 27.13,14 I am confident of this. I will see the goodness of the Lord in the land of the living.

The Lord has promised and I am confident. His promises are coming to pass in the lives of my family and I know he will complete the work he has started, and I will see them all come to the saving knowledge of our wonderful Lord Jesus, my parents, my children and my grandchildren.

When I have had cause to doubt, the Lord has said over and over again.

Isaiah 59:1 Surely the arm of the Lord is not too short to save; nor his ear too dull to hear. Amen.

Chapter 8

The Triangle

When we were married the minister preached a sermon likening Christian marriage to a triangle. Man and wife in each corner and God at the top. As man and wife grow closer to God they grow closer together. Over the years we have seen the out working of this in our lives.

At the beginning of our marriage I had begun my Christian walk and was growing closer to God but Roger was still at the start line. God's amazing grace covered a multitude of things and we loved each other through thick and thin, but we were often pulling in different directions.

1 Corinthians 13.4-8 Love is patient, love is kind. It does not envy, it does not boast, it is not proud. It is not rude, it is not self-seeking, it is not easily angered, it keeps no record of wrongs. Love does not delight in evil but rejoices with the truth. It always protects, always trusts, always hopes, always perseveres. Love never fails.

1 John 3.18 Let us not love with word or tongue but with actions and in truth.

My constant prayer was for Roger to come to the knowledge of Christ's saving power for himself and for our marriage to be totally under God's leadership. Roger had been brought up in a Church of England School and had attended church at various times in his life but he was a very self reliant business man who saw no need for God in his life.

Over the nine years I prayed for his salvation, God showed me that our testimony is not just in what we say but in how we live out our lives, react and deal with circumstances.

Someone, somewhere once said, " I'd rather see a sermon than read one any day" and I believe this to be so true. Our actions often speak far more than anything we could say.

James 1 .22 Do not merely listen to the word and so deceive yourselves. Do what it says.

James 2.18 Show me our faith without deeds, and I will show you my faith by what I do.

God tells us to be a light shining in the darkness drawing others to him.

Philippians 2.14 Do everything without complaining or arguing so that you may become blameless and pure, children of God without fault in a crooked and depraved generation in which you shine like stars in the universe as you hold out the word of life.

The bible also tells us clearly how we are to behave as wives towards our unsaved husbands.

1 Peter 3.1 Wives be submissive to your husbands so that, if any of them do not believe the word, they may be won over without words by the behaviour of their wives.

As well as standing in faith for our loved ones if we talk and act as though they are believers this has a positive effect too. I believe it helps to make them feel included, that God loves them, that He is their God and Father. Even though they have not yet met Him for themselves.

With the help of the Holy Spirit I continued to walk in faith believing on all the promises God had given me for my family.

Hebrews 11.11 He considered Him faithful who had made the promise.

Abraham stood on God's promise. He believed what God had said, even though in the natural it all seemed impossible. How could he a man as good as dead and his wife over eighty years old have a baby? Impossible with man yes. But with God nothing is impossible.

Genesis 18.14 Is anything too hard for the Lord?

Our daughter was the first to be saved at the age of sixteen. Following her salvation we found a church where we could worship and be happy. She and I would go each Sunday and come home so full of joy that Roger decided to come along and try it out for himself. Each week the Holy Spirit softened his heart to receive God's love and forgiveness; Roger's hard shell of self-sufficiency began to crack. Following a bad time in business not knowing which way to turn or what to do all those seeds that had been sown in his heart came to fruition.

The Pastor preached a sermon one evening based on Joshua and the fall of Jericho.

Joshua 6: 2 –5 Then the Lord said to Joshua, "See, I have delivered Jericho into your hands, along with its king and its fighting men. March around the city once with all the armed men. Do this for six days. Make seven priests carry trumpets of rams horns in front of the ark. On the seventh day, march around the city seven times, with the priests blowing the trumpets. When you hear them sound a long blast on the trumpets, make all the people give a loud shout; then the wall of the city will collapse and the people will go up, every man straight in."

Then the Lord said to Joshua, See I have delivered Jericho into our hands........

This spoke into Roger's situation. He felt as though he had been marching around getting nowhere. He knew that he needed to put his complete trust in God and then the walls of his problems would come down like the walls of Jericho. That evening he prayed the prayer of salvation, placing himself and his problems in God's hands. He began to let go and let God.

Matthew 6.25-27 Therefore I tell you, do not worry about your life, what you will eat or drink, or about your body, what you will wear. Is not life more important than food, and body more important than clothes? Look at the birds of the air, they do not sow or reap or store away in barns, and yet your heavenly father feeds them. Are you not much more valuable than they? Who of you by worrying can add a single hour to his life?

From that day onwards Roger's business began to prosper and all the problems began to be resolved. – Praise God.

V33, 34 Seek first His kingdom and His righteousness, and all these things will be given to you.   Therefore do not worry about tomorrow for tomorrow will worry about itself. Each day has enough trouble of its own.

Roger came to the well that will never run dry and as he drank from it he was refreshed, strengthened and renewed. Over the years since as we have put our trust in God to see us through the ups and downs of life we have become closer as a couple. We have both journeyed up the triangle getting closer to God and have become more in love and in tune with each other than ever before.

With God as head of your marriage, your marriage will be happier, stronger; more fulfilled and will withstand the ravages of time. It was His ordination; it is His will and the place where He commands His blessing. 'What God has joined together let no man separate'.

Chapter 9

Do not give up. Stay in faith

Andrew Murray wrote that prayer moves the hand of God. Therefore, whoever and whatever you are praying for, don't give up. Do not get discouraged when the answer doesn't seem to come. So often when we don't see instant results we feel it's not working, it will never happen. Or that God is against us. But the greatest answers come through perseverance, when we keep standing in faith knowing God will answer. Prayers are rather like raindrops watering our seeds of faith, as we continue praying and believing those seeds will grow and we will see the answers.

The Lord tells us to press on in Philippians 3:14 Press on toward the goal to win the prize for which God has called us heavenwards in Christ Jesus. What better prize than to see our loved ones saved.

The Lord calls us to persevere. Hebrews 10: 16 You need to persevere so that when you have done the will of God, you will receive what He has promised. We need to remember what God has promised. Remember the word God gave you. Remember the goal.

We must remember too, no matter how much we may love our husbands, children, and family. God loves them even more. How can we ever deny God's love and desire to see our loved ones saved. Did he not send Jesus, His Son, as an expression of that love?

John 3.16 For God so loved the world that He gave His only Son that whosoever believes upon Him shall not die but have eternal life.

And did Jesus not complete that act of love for each one of us. John 15.13 Greater love has no one than this, that he lay down his life for his friends.

Hebrews 11.1 Now faith is being sure of what we hope for and certain of what we do not see. This is what the ancients were commended for.

v.13 All of them were still living by faith when they died. They did not receive the things promised, they only saw them and welcomed them from a distance.

Keep praying, keep believing, keep trusting, **stay in faith**. God said it and He will do it. Slowly but surely I am seeing all those promises God gave me for my family coming to pass but even if I don't see them I know God is going to bring them about.

Amen

'I believe in the sun even when it is not shining. I believe in love even when I do not feel it. I believe in God even when He is silent.' Anon.

Chapter 10

A defining moment in time

Ezekiel 37 .15 - 19 The word of the Lord came to me; "Son of man, take a stick of wood and write on it. Belonging to Judah and the Israelites associated with him. Then take another stick of wood, and write on it Ephraim's stick, belonging to Joseph and all the house of Israel associated with him. Join them together into one stick so that they will become one in your hand. When your countrymen ask you, Won't you tell us what you mean by this? Say to them. This is what the Sovereign Lord says; I am going to take the stick of Joseph which is in Ephraim's hand – and of the Israelite tribes associated with him, and join it with Judah's stick, making them a single stick of wood, and they will become one in my hand.

Very few times in life can we look back and say that was a defining moment, but for the Goody family our defining moment came in June 1996, at a Pentecost conference in Folkestone Kent.

The conference lead by Ed Silvoso an evangelist from Argentina, focused on Unity within the Church and how the dividing walls within the Church, and within each of us, needed to be broken for God to use us all for His purpose and Glory. How we would be a stronger force to be reckoned with if we stood together to reach our community for Christ. At the end of the meetings the Lord gave me the above scripture of the two sticks. One of the sticks being the Goody family and the other being Pastor Robert Maasbach and the Life Church in Folkestone. I knew that in some way we were going to be joined by the Lord and through that joining the Lord would do wondrous things. So strongly did I feel about it that I went outside the conference hall and found a stick broke it in half and gave one half to Pastor Robert together with the above scripture and kept the other half myself.

It was at this conference that our son aged eight gave his life to the Lord.

At this time we were living in Essex and we would come to Folkestone occasionally to visit family and the Life Church. Every time we visited Pastor Robert would welcome us and ask us when we were moving to Kent. This was not something we could easily see happening. Roger's business was in London and it would be very difficult to operate it from Kent. I was involved with teaching Horse Riding to the Disabled and we were raising funds for a riding facility at our local Children's Hospice, which we thought we would be running. I had also just started working part time for a funeral company as a funeral arranger. Our children were all settled with their schooling and friends and our elderly parents who relied on us lived close by. We were also involved with our local church helping in the Sunday School, Alpha Group, House Group etc. It didn't seem possible for us to move or that the Lord wanted us to move. I began to think the word regarding the sticks was possibly for our churches to join together in someway, not for us. We were too busy serving God and family at home in Essex.

It can be easy sometimes to twist God's word to suit our own agenda and this is what we did.
However -

Isaiah 14.24 The Lord Almighty has sworn, "Surely, as I have planned, so it will be, and as I have purposed, so it will stand.

The Lord will watch over His word to perform it and it will accomplish what He desires.

Isaiah 55.11 My word that goes out from my mouth. It will not return to me empty, but will accomplish what I desire and achieve the purpose for which I sent it.

I am sure the Lord must get so frustrated with us at times, as we continually ignore His word to us and carry on in our own sweet way. We pray and seek His will and say Lord use me, I am yours ready to do your will. Show me what you would have me do. Then when he shows us we take no notice.

It is at these times the Lord has to take action to make us take notice. Shout to get us to hear.

Roger's business faced financial ruin and we had to sell our beautiful four bed roomed detached house in the best part of town and move to a small semi with just enough room to swing a cat. It was said to us then. " Aren't you moving to Folkestone?" Our reply was. "No that's not for us".

Although we enjoyed serving God at our local church we knew there was something missing and felt like we were in a cage spiritually. We knew there was more and were hungry for God's will in our life and family.

Finally God opened our eyes. We had just raised over £25,000 for the riding facility at the Children's Hospice and plans were underway for more fundraising events. Our goal was within our sights and we were looking forward to opening the stables and seeing the children enjoy the facilities. Then we received a letter from the organisers saying they did not wish us to raise any more money. The money raised would be held on account until such time they decided how to use it. May be for a riding facility or may be not. Our authority to raise money in their name was taken away.

To say we were very upset doesn't begin to describe our feelings. It was not just all the work we had put in and all the money we had raised. It was the excitement at seeing the stables built and the children enjoying it. It was all the people who had really got behind our vision for the whole project who would be disappointed that really upset us. It was as though the carpet had been pulled out from under our feet. It was gone. We couldn't understand it; we thought it was what God had called us to do. What had we done wrong?

After a very tearful sleepless night, we received in the post the next day a note scribbled on a compliments slip, from Pastor Robert in Folkestone on which was written these words.

Do not seek the praise of man. Seek the Lord, who is well pleased with what you have done.

Pastor Robert had no idea of what we were going through, infact he knew very little about us at all, so we knew that the word came directly from the Lord. We were reminded of the two sticks and knew instantly that we had to move to Kent to join with Life Church, as God had told us to do nearly two years ago.

Zechariah 6: 15 Those who are far away will come and help to build the temple of the Lord, and you will know that the Lord Almighty has sent me to you. This will happen if you diligently obey the Lord your God.

As we prayed about and put into action our plans to move, God confirmed His word over and over again, giving us the strength and courage to put our hand in His and make the move we thought impossible.

Isaiah 43.18 Forget the former things. Do not dwell on the past. See, I am doing a new thing. Now it spring up; do you not perceive it?

Isaiah 45.2 I will go before you and will level the mountains. I will break down gates of bronze and cut through bars of iron. I will give you treasures of darkness, riches stored in secret places, so that you may know that I am the Lord.

'Perfect submission, all is at rest, I in my Saviour am happy and blest; Watching and waiting, looking above. Filled with His goodness, lost in His love. ' - Fanny J. Crosby

Chapter 11

The Move

Genesis 12. 1 – 3 The Lord had said to Abram, "Leave your country, your people and your father's household and go to the land I will show you. I will make you into a great nation and I will bless you; I will make your name great, and you will be a blessing. I will bless those who bless you, and whoever curses you I will curse; and all peoples on earth will be blessed through you."

We moved to Kent in July 1998 and have never looked back. As soon as we had placed our hand in the Lord's things happened fast. Our house was sold in a few months and a new one found. Roger made the necessary arrangements to transfer his office to our new home, and I managed to arrange a job transfer from the funeral service in Essex where I worked to Kent. Our eldest son was offered a place at the local technical college to do mechanics and also a part time job as an apprentice mechanic with a local garage.

In the September of this year Life Church began Oakwood School. Christian education for students aged 4 – 18. Our youngest son was one of the first students to attend and graduated eight years later with a Grade 3 in Christian Schools Education, which was sufficient qualification to get him in to University to study music. The wonderful environment within Oakwood School and the Christian teaching, enabled our son to excel and grow in to a confident God filled young man, and we are so grateful to God for bringing us to Kent for this alone.

However the first year in our new home and church was very challenging.

Roger was trying to establish himself and prove to his business associates that he was still up and running, open for business. His office had always been in London and so to move it out into the country was indeed a challenge. Communications had to be installed at home, telex machines, fax machines, telephones, computers etc. As well as trying to run his business Roger had to take our son to school and pick him up as I was working full time. This took a good hour out of the office each day and put quite a strain on him.

Our daughter had decided not to move with us but remain in Essex and was finding life hard on her own and we all missed her terribly.

Settling in to our new church was difficult. Everything was strange, the people, the hymns, the way the service was conducted. It was all different.

I found working full time as well as trying to settle into our new home and church difficult. I can remember sitting in my office wondering why the Lord had called us to Kent, all we both seemed to do was work to try and make ends meet. What had he called us for? Due to the nature of my job, I often had quiet times in my day when I was able to spend time with the Lord reading my Bible and praying. One particularly gloomy day I can remember sitting looking out of the window thinking, what was it all about, when I happened to glance at my daily reading. It read – Two men looked through prison bars, one saw sand the other stars. I then heard God's voice asking me, what do you see Katherine? Are you just looking at the sand, at all the difficulties or are you looking at the stars, at me and what I am going to do? I realised then I had let my focus slip, I had taken my eyes off Jesus.

Turn your eyes upon Jesus look full in His wonderful face and the things of earth will grow strangely dim in the light of His Glory and Grace.

Be still, and know that I am God; Psalm 46.10

My soul, waits silently for God alone. For my expectation is from Him. Psalm 62.5

The Lord will fulfil his purpose for me. Psalm 138.8

Drop Thy still dews of quietness, till all our strivings cease; take from our souls the strain and stress, and let our ordered lives confess the beauty of Thy peace. –John G Whittier.

Chapter 12

I can do all things through Him who gives me strength

Psalm 91:16 With long life will I satisfy them and show them my salvation.

The funeral home where I worked held death awareness classes to advise people of what to do when someone died, what to expect and all the things that needed to be done. The idea was to take the fear out of the unknown and make the process easier for people when the time came. As well as the general public, staff from doctors surgeries and Residential Care Homes came as part of their training. During these sessions I would have opportunity to chat with some of the staff from the care homes and I heard many sad stories of how they had experienced old people unable to sleep for fear of dieing. How they would sit up in bed willing themselves to stay awake so they would not die in their sleep. This really upset me and I began to pray to the Lord asking him how we could help.

Praise God that the majority of funerals I arranged were for the elderly. For people who had reached the end of their years naturally. Sadly though, this often left a husband or wife alone wondering whether they would see their partners again. It amazed me how so many people had not given God a thought until it was too late. In the office we had a large cupboard where the ashes from cremations were kept prior to despatch. One day, whilst looking for some ashes I felt the Lord speak to me, His voice coming from within the cupboard. He said very clearly. "I do not want my people to end up this way." At that moment I knew exactly who He was talking about and what He wanted us to do. He wanted us to go to the old people and tell them about the good news of salvation before it was too late.

Roger and I prayed about this and sought the Lord on how it could be done. From this the idea to go to the residential homes came, to do a Sunday praise service. Roger playing his guitar with me singing hymns and choruses. It's amazing out of all the gifts I thought God had given me singing wasn't one of them. Roger was great at playing the guitar, but me sing, no way. The thought of standing in front of others was not something I could do either, you'd be lucky if I would say hello let alone sing and speak. But we soon found out that when God calls, He equips. He gives us His strength and courage, His ability.

Philippians 4:13 I can do everything through him who gives me strength.

2 Corinthians 12:9 My grace is sufficient for you, for my power is made perfect in weakness.

With God's voice clearly in my mind I approached Pastor Robert at Life Church and told him of the Lord's instruction. He was overjoyed and said that he had been praying for a long time for someone to join with him to minister to the elderly. We were given the Lords blessing to go reach the elderly for Christ.

How to begin was our next problem. We looked in the telephone directory and there were so many residential homes we didn't know where to start. So we picked twelve and wrote them a letter, saying we were from the Life Church in Folkestone and wondered if the residents would enjoy a Sunday afternoon praise service, sing some hymns and songs?

After two weeks we had not received one reply. So feeling bold, I picked up the phone to the first four on the list asking them if they had received our letter and whether they would be interested. Each one said yes and how much they thought the residents would enjoy it, particularly those who were unable to get out to church. We had our first four Sunday afternoons booked. This was the birth of Autumn Harvest. A ministry given by God to serve those of senior years.

Chapter 13

Amazing Grace how sweet the sound

It's so amazing to see the Lord at work, especially when it's in you. I said earlier when God calls us to do something, He will equip, strengthen and give courage, but it's one thing to say it and another to believe it. So it was with great trepidation Roger and I went to our first Residential Home to do a Sunday afternoon Service. I can remember walking into the residents lounge, all the dear old people were sitting in a circle looking at us, and I thought to myself there is no way I can speak, let along sing. As Roger began to play I tentively started to sing Amazing Grace, and as I sang I looked to my right and there was a lady crying. Oh no I thought are we that bad?? But no, as we continued to play and sing she began to join in, and at then end of the service the matron explained that the lady was blind and so missed going to church, they were tears of happiness not sadness. That afternoon the matron who was a catholic was so touched by the Lord, she asked us for prayer. She had a stomach growth which she feared was cancer, and was going to the hospital the next day for tests. Roger and I prayed with her and said we would continue to pray and believe for her complete healing in Jesus name. Later that week she phoned us so excited, to say that the Lord had answered our prayers and the growth had gone and she hadn't got cancer.

Hebrews 2:4 God testified to it by signs, wonders and various miracles.

It didn't matter to the Lord that we couldn't do it, that I couldn't sing and felt so ill equipped. He can do all things; he just needs willing vessels to work through. All he needed was our obedience to go and He did the rest. By our going Jesus was able to minister to the residents and bring healing to the Matron. It is not what we can do but what the Holy Spirit can do through us.

Psalm 63:7 Because you are my help, I sing in the shadow of your wings.

Zechariah 4:6 Not by might nor by power, but by my spirit says the Lord Almighty.

The Lord confirmed His word to us by signs and wonders and gave us the courage and the confidence to carry on and as we did we saw the light of God's love break through the darkness.

The second home we visited was a challenge, as soon as we went in the door the smell hit you. The smell of urine and dinner, so overpowering was it that it made you want to be sick. We felt like turning straight round and going home. The staff showed us into the lounge and left us to it. Sitting round the room in semi darkness were about ten old folk, sitting in varying states of disarray. Some were asleep, others dribbling and staring into space. We were overwhelmed and cried out to the Lord, Oh Lord why have you brought us here, what can we do??? The Lord told us to just start singing and playing the hymns and as we did so very slowly the people began to wake up, come alive and the room started to brighten. You could feel the heaviness lift and the light of God's presence fill the room. Eventually people began to join in and sing and by the time we left many of them were sitting up smiling and talking. God had bought his gift of life again just through our obedience.

From then onwards our hearts were filled with God's love for all the residents in the homes. His heart became our hearts, his love became our love, it became our passion to take His love into the homes and see him bring joy, peace, love and hope. See Him heal, strengthen and encourage. Today, some eighteen years on Autumn Harvest is still ministering in and around the Folkestone area, holding services and ministering to the residents through visiting and activities. Praise God for all that He has done and all that He is going to do as we continue to take Jesus into the Homes.. The scripture He gave us is coming to pass. Psalm 91.16 With long life will I satisfy him and show him my salvation.

He has satisfied them with long life and He is showing them His salvation. Praise God. Amen.

Chapter 14

A New Challenge

Matthew 8:18-22 When Jesus saw the crowd around him; he gave orders to cross to the other side of the lake. Then a teach of the law came to him and said, "Teacher, I will follow you wherever you go." Jesus replied, "Foxes have holes and birds of the air have nests, but the Son of Man has nowhere to lay his head". Another disciple said to him, "Lord, first let me go and bury my father." But Jesus told him, "Follow me, and let the dead bury their own dead."

In September 1999, one year after our move to Kent the Lord called me to go to bible school. The School of Life and Ministry at Life Church, Folkestone. This was a full time course for two years. So a big commitment for the family and me. I would need to give much of my time to prayer and study, as well as attending classes, leaving Roger to carry many of my job's as housewife and mother. School fees needed to be found and as I needed to leave my job this was an added worry. Would we be able to manage financially? Should I put pressure on Roger as he tried to build his business? Was it fair to ask the family to go without things so I could go to Bible school? These were all questions I asked myself and the Lord.

Psalm 25:4-6 Show me your ways, O Lord, teach me your paths; guide me in your truth and teach me, for you are God my Saviour, and my hope is in you all day long.

Reading the above scripture from Matthew 8 gave me my answer. To truly follow Jesus we must be prepared to give up everything as he gave up everything for us. He didn't say it would be easy but he did say:

Luke 18:29-30 "I tell you the truth, no one who has left home or wife or brothers or parents or children for the sake of the kingdom of God, will fail to receive many times as much in this age and in the age to come, eternal life."

Matthew 10:37-39 Anyone who loves his father or mother more than me is not worthy of me; anyone who loves his son or daughter more than me is not worthy of me, and anyone who does not take up his cross and follow me is not worthy of me. Whoever finds his life will lose it, and whoever loses his life for my sake will find it.

Psalm 25:12-13 He will instruct him in the way chosen for him. He will spend his days in prosperity and his descendants will inherit the land.

Psalm 37:5-6 Commit your way to the Lord; trust in him and he will do this. He will make your righteousness shine like the dawn, the justice of your cause like the noonday sun.

Proverbs 2:1-10 If you accept my words and store up my commands within you, turning your ear to wisdom and applying your heart to understanding, and if you call out for insight and cry aloud for understanding, and if you look for it as for silver and search for it as for hidden treasure, then you will understand the fear of the Lord and find the knowledge of God. For the Lord gives wisdom, and from his mouth comes knowledge and understanding. He holds victory in store for the upright, he is a shield to those whose walk is blameless, for he guards the course of the just and protects the way of his faithful ones. Then you will understand what is right and just and fair. For wisdom will enter your heart, and knowledge will be pleasant to your soul.

With the family's support and knowing that the Lord would meet all our needs I began two of the most exciting and challenging years of my life.

Chapter 15

Renewing the Mind

Proverbs 9:10 The fear of the Lord is the beginning of wisdom, and knowledge of the Holy One is understanding.

Over the two years I spent at Bible School, through teaching, study and prayer I came to a greater knowledge of the vastness of God's love for His children. Of how much that love can change us if we surrender our lives and will to God and of how we can change the lives of those around us by being Jesus here on earth.

One of the first studies we did was called renewing the mind, on which we had to produce a 2,000 word essay. It really put's in to a nutshell all that we believe in as born again Christians.

Renewing the mind

'In the beginning God created the heavens and the earth.' God created the world and all that is in it. He made it beautiful, perfect and completely without flaw. 'And God saw that it was good.' Then God said, "Let Us make man in Our image, according to Our likeness." So God formed man out of the dust of the ground and breathed into his nostrils the breath of life, and man became a living being.

Formed of the dust of the ground refers to mans body. Breathed into his nostrils is the breath of life and refers to mans spirit as it came from God.

Man is made up of three parts. Spirit, soul and body. The body is what we see, our flesh made from the dust of the earth. Our world consciousness. The spirit is the life. There are two spirits, our own spirit and Gods spirit. At creation God breathed His spirit of life in to us and His spirit and ours were one. God consciousness. The soul is a combination of spirit and body, a place where the two meet. It is the site of mans personality and influence, of our individuality. Self consciousness. At creation the spirit was created to be the, 'General of our being.' The soul made to be the, 'Commander,' obeying the leading of the General. The body was made to be a, 'foot soldier,' doing what the soul tells it. It was Gods intention that the spirit rule over man. The spirit of God at one with man. Adam would have known nothing of the strivings of the flesh that we have, as his spirit was entirely one with God.

The soul reflecting this in the way he acted and lived. E.g. Genesis 2:25 'And they were both naked, the man and his wife, and were not ashamed.'

God made man very different from all the other created beings. He gave us perfect freedom. He did not make us to be automatically controlled by His will but gave us free will, freedom of choice. Therefore we had the choice to either obey Gods commands or disobey them. Consent to the devils schemes or not consent.

At creation God planted a garden in Eden where He put Adam. The garden was full of beautiful plants and trees pleasing to the eye and good to eat. Adam had everything he desired and he lived in harmony with God, communing with God, spirit to spirit. In the middle of the garden was the tree of life and the tree of knowledge of good and evil. God commanded Adam saying, "Of every tree of the garden you may freely eat but of the tree of knowledge of good and evil you shall not eat, for in the day that you eat of it you shall surely die."

It was Gods desire that Adam was happy, and so that he was not alone God made him a helper, companion, Eve. Eve was called a woman because she was taken out of man, Adam. They lived together in unity with God until Eve was tempted by the serpent, Satan. He deceived her in to eating from the tree of knowledge. Deceived herself she gave the fruit from the tree of knowledge also to Adam, consequently cutting themselves off from God. their spirit was no longer connected to Gods spirit, hence they were spiritually dead. This was the death God had spoken of when he had warned them not to eat of the tree knowledge. A spiritual death. If Eve's mind had been controlled by her spirit she would have rejected the temptation of the serpent. However because she exercised her free will she disobeyed God. The order that God had created in man of Spirit, Soul, and Body had been reversed. No longer did the spirit reign, but now the body with all its lusts and desires ruled. The Body ruling over the spirit, meeting in the soul, corrupting all our emotions, desires, changing the way we think and act. Turning us from God lead people into self lead people. One of the first emotions man felt was shame. Adam and Eve hid in the garden from God as they knew they had done wrong and disobeyed Him. They became self conscious and covered themselves. Other effects of self consciousness are guilt, blame, hate, anger, anxiety, worry and doubt. They tried to hide their self consciousness. All these things lead to self destruction, death. They are opposite to Gods will.

The consequence of Adam and Eve disobeying God was that they separated all mankind from God. Death began to reign, not only in mankind but in the world itself, because the spirit of God had left them . When they died as they would through the death and decay that was now in the world, they would return to the dust from which they had come. Cut off from the life giving spirit of God they began to die. The free will God had given man chose to disobey God. This is sin. From then on the body ruled, we obeyed self not God.

Adam and Eve continued on after the fall. Their spirits as well as the spirits of all their descendants fell under the oppression of the soul. Gradually the soul and the spirit merged, everything then done according to intellect or feeling. Man still had a spirit but it was dead to God. In giving in to its passions and lusts the soul becomes a slave to the body or flesh as it is often called. Even in mans search for God all was done by the strength and will of mans soul, their was no revelation of Gods spirit. Man was not in tune with God anymore but received the corrupted wisdom of Satan. All Satan's wisdom was entirely opposite to Gods.

Nothing previously had experienced anything like death or decay, Adam and Eve knew nothing of good and evil until they ate from the tree of knowledge, and with this knowledge came a huge responsibility. They had to be their own moral judge. Gods intention was that we lived in the glory of God, he had wanted to sit on the throne of our hearts and judge for us, but now man was left to make up his own mind. Our conscience is our moral judge and everyone's is different. Left to his own desires man began to mess up big time. The world became a corrupt and evil place, the effects of sin irreparable. Man continues to fall deeper and deeper into sin and God was sorry that He had made man on the earth. He decided to destroy the human race and start over again , with a single family, that of Noah, who was a good man and walked with God. So God flooded the earth leaving nothing except Noah, his family and the animals with him in the ark. Here we begin to see Gods intent to restore what had been lost through Adam and Eves disobedience .

At the fall Gods restoration work began immediately. The self conscious Adam and Eve tried to make coverings for their nakedness by the work of their own hands. However, God provided clothing for them made from animal skin, clearly revealing His plan of redemption and restoration. Again in the story of Cain and Abel, God showed that the issue of a blood sacrifice was essential for right standing with Him. Cain's vegetable offering was the fruit of his own efforts and was unacceptable to God, but Abel's offering of a blood sacrifice was pleasing to God. All through the Old Testament the people tried to restore themselves to God. God gave His laws to the people through Moses. They were to act as an attendant to mankind. Galatians 3:24 the law was our tutor. They were to cause man to strive for perfection. To produce a consciousness of sin and compel man to seek salvation. The law was part of God eternal plan for mankind. They were asked for by the children of Israel. To expose our sin, not making man sin, but showing man he is a sinner. To reveal sin. Sin is the nature of what we are and sins are what we do. Gods original plan for man was that we should live out of our God consciousness, walk according to the law automatically. Man tries to justify himself, but the more he tries the more he fails. Man continually fails to meet the mark, and as soon as he steps outside Gods boundary line, he sins. Through the prophets man recognised the need of salvation, they knew it was at hand and would soon be revealed. Isaiah 56:1 My salvation is about to come.

Right from the start God showed the necessity of blood sacrifice, but no animal can pay the penalty of mans sin. Only humanity can atone for humanity. The sacrifice has to be pure, without sin and no man was without sin. Therefore God sent His only Son the Lord Jesus to provide for our salvation. Praise God!

Romans 8:3 For what the law could not do in that it weak through the flesh, God did by sending His own Son in the likeness of sinful flesh.

John 3: 16 For God so loved the world that He gave His only Son that whosoever believed in Him shall not perish but have eternal life.

Through Jesus death on the cross he paid the price for the sins of humanity. Taking upon himself our punishment , opening the way for us to restore our relationship with God. John 5:24 He who believes in Him shall be judged no more. Through one man Adam, sin came into the world, and through one man Jesus, our sins are forgiven. Jesus blood cleanses us from our sins and His resurrection restores our union with God. 2 Corinthians 5:17 Therefore if anyone is in Christ he is a new creation, old things have passed away, behold all things have become new. The old man has died with Christ and we are born again by Gods spirit into the resurrection life. John 3:3 Unless one is born again he cannot see the kingdom of God. It is here Gods spirit returns to us. Our spirit witnesses with His spirit that we are children of God. He is our Heavenly Father.

When we recognise that we have been crucified with Christ and it is no longer I who live, but Christ who lives in me, and the life which I now live in the flesh I live by faith in the Son of God. Galatians 2:20 We begin to see the desire of God at creation being restored.

That we are lead by the spirit again and not by the body/flesh. Our souls are restored.

We are born fleshly. It cannot please God. It is an enemy of God. It corrupts. It is weak. It profits nothing. It cannot be justified. It brings forth the fruit of death. Serves sin. It is condemned. It cannot be righteous. It cannot be in the spirit. It cannot experience the glory of God. It cannot inherit the Kingdom of God. It is filthy. It is full of temptation. It persecutes the spirit. It reaps corruption. It is unreliable. It is deadly. We need to hate it. Despise it. It cannot be changed, it needs to die. We cannot combat sin in the flesh, only through staying in the spirit. Colossians 3:1 Seek those things that are above. Our flesh needs to be crucified with Christ. Romans 6:11 Dead to sin, alive in Christ. The blood of Jesus cannot cleanse our flesh. Flesh can only die to sin. Go through the cross. Sins are conquered instantly at Calvary and we have our salvation, but self or our flesh is conquered daily.

Satan wants to undermine our believing ability, question our position in Christ. We need to be sure of our position, of what God has done for us. That, 'Nothing can separate us from the love of God.' Absolutely nothing. We don't need to just cope. Jesus came to give us life in abundance, freedom. We stay free from the realms of darkness by living and staying in the Heavenly realm. Walking in the spirit helps us stay in this position. We cannot walk in the lusts of the flesh if we want to stay in the Heavenly realm. By the work of Christ, by our position in him, the door is open to this Kingdom. It is impossible to have one foot in the Heavenly realm and one foot in the world. We need to learn to fully give ourselves over to the spirit and stay there. God wants not only our spirit to walk in this realm but our Soul also. Our Soul needs to experience the cross. The cross needs to go through our entire being, we need to step through the door the cross opens.

The Soul is where our will is and our emotions. The 'I'. Where we choose Gods will or our will. Whether to be led by the spirit or by the body/flesh. Many times we operate our lives out of our soul, serving God on our terms, or by how we feel. Those who walk according to the soul follow their own desires, not Gods. Often seeking sensual pleasure, utterly dependent on their feelings, prideful and self serving. They are self serving, pursue mental wisdom, are easily moved, over sensitive, boast in their humility, crave works, are easily discouraged in their actions, experts in finding fault, act from impulse rather than principle, they possess mountains of opinions and oceans of plans. They seek prominent position in spiritual work, they experience unspeakable joy whenever recognised or accepted, are extremely ambitious, take great pride in the smallest of success. Often abundantly gifted and often spend more time calculating than in prayer. Our soul/self must die. It is Gods intention that our soul be led by the spirit. For the spirit to be the largest part of us. We want to live out of our inner man, sure of what we believe in the spirit. If we want to live correctly, we need to die correctly. The soul needs to come into alignment with our spirit, subject to the spirit not the flesh. Not out of our strength, but through Christ in me. We need to let go and let God. rest in God. Stay in the rest, believing and trusting, adhering to the word of God.

Praise God for Jesus. 1 Corinthians 15:57 We have the victory through our Lord Jesus Christ. We can do all things through Christ who strengthens us. We just need to follow Him, keep our eyes on Him. God didn't leave us alone to struggle but gave us His Holy spirit to help us. The only way to experience the resurrection life is to stay in Christ crucified, continually. Take up the cross daily. The cross must touch our Body, Soul and Spirit until we again restore the order as God had planned to Spirit, Soul and Body. There is nothing we can do to obtain this victory, it is a gift of grace from God.

We need to completely surrender our lives to God. Not my will but yours Father, in all areas of our lives. Our family, finances, partner, intellect, pursuit of wisdom, giftings, health, our own good works, time etc. We need to be careful of self reliance and self confidence. Phillipians 3:3 Put no confidence in the flesh. The only security we have is Jesus, He is our confidence. Following Jesus brings us a rest and inner peace. We need to know we are being lead by Him and trust Him. Look unto Jesus the author and finisher of our faith. Experience the road to the cross as we turn our self life over to

God. Submit our will to Gods will, not our will but Gods will. As we surrender all self to God we can often feel lost and alone, but it is here we learn to rely totally on God. We mustn't give up here, we must experience it, press on to receive the prize set before us in Christ Jesus. God has a perfect plan for our lives and those we love, this can only be achieved if we let go and let God, see His will not ours. Our emotions will try and get in the way, but we must not be lead by them, but by the spirit which will show us the will of God. God only wants the best for us, He loves us, we are His children. All things work together for good.

Jesus lead a life completely surrended to God. He lived not for his will but for the will of the Father. As a child he sort to do the Fathers business. At his Baptism to fulfil all righteousness. Throughout his ministry, 'My meat is to do the will of Him who sent me.' 'I came to do the will of the Father.' 'Lo I have come to do thy will.' He surrended his life unto death in the Garden of Gethsemane. 'Not as I will, but as You will.' This needs to be our desire, to surrender our lives unto death and to live out, not my will but yours Father.

Sin came into the world in the Garden of Eden and man was cut off from the spirit of life in God. In the garden of Gethsemane Jesus surrended his life for us that we may be restored to our Father in Heaven and have the spirit of God again living within us. That we can become again Spirit beings, lead by the spirit of God enjoying all its benefits. That death holds no place for us, we are alive again through Jesus who has set us free.

I am the Alpha and the Omega, the beginning and the end. Revelations 1:8

When I read that now, I can't believe that I wrote it, but yes, my greatest work, by Katherine Goody, and that was just in the first few months of Bible School. Over the two years the Lord truly established His word deep in my heart. I amazed myself by the revelations He showed me and in the things He enabled me to do.

49

None more so than when I went on my first mission trip in 2000 to India.

During the nine years of our marriage I had opportunity to travel to many different countries and encouraged by Roger's love and support I begun to do many things that I had thought impossible. So when God asked me to go on a missions trip to India without Roger it was a big step for us both. Two weeks in a foreign land away from my strength and support, Roger, but God wanted to show me that He was my true strength and support. I can remember praying and seeking God's answer as to whether I should go to India, part of me wishing that He would say no, but then wanting to experience everything God had for me. One of my prayers was for the finance of the trip to be met without Roger paying for it. Bearing in mind I had no savings of my own, this was quite a tall order. I prayed and left it in the Lord's hands. Someone sent me a small donation of £10, but I had a long way to go to reach the £1200 needed for the trip. One of the teachers at Bible school told me that the rest of the money would come, to stay in faith and believe. The £10 was the first seed and it would grow and accomplish that which God had planned. God never starts something without finishing it, he assured me. Well sure enough the money came. In a way that I would never have expected. Tall order? I should have known better. Earlier that year my dear Uncle Stan had passed away and unknown to myself he had left me a small amount of money in his will. The amount was £1000. During the second World War Uncle Stan had been stationed in India, during which time he had developed a great love of the country and its people. So when the money was sent to me, I knew that he would have been so happy and proud for me to use the money to pay for the missions trip to India.

Chapter 16

The Mission Field

On my trip to India in 2000 and consequently the following year to Nepal I experienced just how wide and how deep the Father's love is for the whole world. It is not restricted by our limited vision but reaches out to the darkest and most remote parts of the world. To an Indian child begging on the streets, to families living in a village in a house no bigger than a shed, without fresh food or water. To those sleeping on the streets, alone and abused.

Who could ever imagine, that God would call two young women from the UK to climb up the Himalayan Mountains of Nepal, to the remote villages and forgotten people of the world, to tell them that He Loved them. For that is what He did with two girls from the missions trip I was on to Nepal.

From there He birthed the vision of the RANCH. Remote Area of Nepal Children's Home. A home where families could send their children to be educated and raised in the Christian Faith, with the ultimate vision of the children returning to witness and teach their own families and villages. A home where the children could live in safety and health, well fed and loved.

In the remote villages there is extreme poverty, no health care, no schools. As soon as the children are old enough they work on the land with their parents. Large families are the norm and often parents will give their child to a monastery, or send them out to fend for themselves, as they cannot afford to keep them.

The vision came to fruition, and the RANCH welcomed its first children in 2002. In 2003 and 2004 Roger and I had the chance to visit The Ranch together and be part of the work God was doing there. We had the wonderful opportunity to teach not only the children, but the workers too, of a life lived with Christ. We were able to support and encourage them, to remind them that they were not alone and that there were people praying for them and thinking of them at all times.

Working on the missions field certainly opens your eyes to see what is important in life. You see that having as much as we do in the West, money, cars, houses, clothes etc. doesn't bring us true happiness and contentment. It is in knowing Jesus that we are truly rich. When we live in peace, and love with joy in our hearts, thankful for the simple things of life, friendship, sunshine, a soft bed to sleep on and a full stomach. It made me realise too that our true strength and support comes solely from the Lord. He is all we need and will meet all our needs.

'When we are in a situation where Jesus is all we have we soon discover He is all we really need.'
Gig Graham Ichividjian

Chapter 17

The RANCH

These next paragraphs are taken from the journal from our second trip to the RANCH in 2004.

Arrived Kathmandu Saturday 15ᵗʰ May. Booked in to the Aloha Inn for our over night stop in Kathmandu before flying on to Pokhara. We can't wait to see all the children again, and meet the new arrivals. Half hour flight to Pokhara with Buddha airaways. Felt a bit like Indiana Jones in Raiders of the lost ark!! Arrived safely at hotel Shangrila. Were informed on arrival that the Maoists had bombed the Fish Tail Lodge that day and the hotel had to be closed. Praise God we nearly stayed there.

Went to the RANCH Sunday evening and received a very noisy welcome. The children all wanted to be hugged at the same time they nearly knocked us over. It was so good to see them all again. They had all grown so much. Immediately you could see how happy they all were and how God had bought a peace and contentment to their lives. The uncertainty and emptiness that was in their eyes had gone and they had a special sparkle. The new children were just as enthusiastic to see us and we soon made lots of new friends.

They were so pleased with all the clothes we were able to take. Praise God for everyone who gave. Without these gifts the children would not have any clothes or only very few. There was something for everyone, they all have a new set of clothes which they wear to church and a set of play clothes.

We had planned to go to the RANCH each day to spend time and share Gods word with the adults and with the children when they came home from school. But plans are made to be broken as always. We learnt that there was to be a transport strike due to the Maoist activity and the political situation. Managed to hire some bikes and prayed that the Lord would give us the strength to cycle to the RANCH. About five miles each way, help!! Unfortunately Roger ate something dodgy and had a bad bout of food poisoning so we were unable to go anywhere. (Perhaps it was the Lord's answer to my cry of help, with the cycling.) After a few days he was a bit better so we braved the cycle , up hill most of the way in 40 degrees heat. Arrived hot and sweaty after about 45 minutes. Not too bad since I hadn't been on a bike for over a year. Homeward bound it was a little easier on the legs but the monsoon rains had started and we arrived back at the hotel like a couple of drowned rats.

The new children at the RANCH had only been there a few weeks and we had expected them to be very rough and ready. But you would have thought they had been there months. They were very well behaved and obedient. They had adapted very well to the discipline of the home and settled in happily. All played well with each other most of the time. A wonderful job had been done laying down the ground rules etc. for both staff and children. It is certainly a home built on the Lord's foundation, filled with His peace, joy and love.

On the whole the new children are reasonably healthy. A few skin problems due to the change of climate etc. quite a few nits, which was a challenge for me when I was asked to do some hair cuts. But praise God He protected us and kept the itchy things away.

The children are doing well at school, some of them are very bright. They are learning to read and write in Nepali, Tibetan and English. Puts us to shame in the UK when most of us only speak English. They are all at The Good Shepherd Medium School run by Dolma and her husband. They also run a home for about 60 Tibetan children and have church as well.

Despite the Maoists activities, heat and rain we were able to spend time sharing God's word with the house parents and children.

One afternoon we had a real breakthrough with the house parents. We had been sharing and talking about being one in Christ, about serving one another in love. The Lord led us to the passage in John chapter 13 where Jesus washes His disciples feet. We felt that this was what He wanted us to do, so we all washed each others feet. It certainly broke any barriers between us and we had a great time of sharing. They were asking lots of questions and we were able to encourage them in the Lord. From this time a bond was made between us, a oneness.

Before we left we had opportunity to preach at Dolma's church. We preached about Jesus the light of the world. How we are called to shine for Jesus, like stars in the universe. Philippians 2: v.15,16 Shine like stars in the universe as you hold out the word of life. How too like Brother Yun, the Heavenly Man, a Chinese Missionary, they were to take the gospel back to their villages and into all the world. Praise God his word ministered to them greatly and was a climax to the teaching they had already been studying. God never ceases to amaze us. He goes before us and prepares the way when we walk with Him. It so encouraged us to know that we had got it right and given them what the Lord had wanted them to hear.

The light of the gospel is beginning to shine in the darkness in Nepal. We have come back very much aware of the needs and problems the people in Nepal face. Not only at the RANCH but in daily life in Nepal, with the political situations and the Maoist Activities. We thank God He chose to send us to be part of His work in Nepal and to encourage them. We would also encourage others to step out and do something for missions. Sometimes the work can seem so huge that we think, what difference can we make? But with God's help we can make a difference to the lives of those he draws us to, and ultimately to the bigger picture. Just think if someone hadn't shared God's love with Billy Graham he wouldn't have been able to reach all those millions of people he has with the gospel of Christ. It isn't always about the going it is in the giving and supporting that we can make a difference too. Give it a try we guarantee you will be blessed.

Matthew 10:8 Freely you have received, freely give.

Chapter 18

Do not forget to Entertain Strangers

Hebrews 13:2 Do not forget to entertain strangers, for by so doing some people have entertained angels without know it.

In 2004 Roger went to Bible school where he met Jeton, a young man from Kosovo. This young man and his family had been badly affected by the war between the Albanians and the Serbs, he had lost his father and many other relatives, but Praise God through the love of Christ and the message of the Gospel he was overcoming his hurts and fears. Jeton came to live with us during his time at Bible School and we came to love him as a son and he became part of our family. After graduation when he returned to Kosovo, we said goodbye to him with sadness but also with joy, that he was returning better equipped to handle his family situation and also to share the love of Christ with others in his country. We continued to support him and his family and then in 2005 we had the opportunity to visit and work along side him in his church and ministry. Whilst we were there we met a young man by the name of Albert, he was our driver during our visit and worked in the ministry with Jeton. He had a true servants heart and his greatest desire was to serve Christ. He loved music, and enjoyed playing the guitar and leading worship. The Lord spoke to us telling us that Albert should come to visit the UK and Life Church, so we invited him. Consequently he came the following year and went to Bible School at Life Church, Folkestone. Under the teaching he received he grew in stature in the Lord and has now returned to Kosovo to plant a church.

Mark 9:41 I tell you the truth anyone who gives you a cup of water in my name because you belong to Christ will certainly not lose his reward.

The reason I am telling this story is that in life God often wants to use us to fulfil his plans and purposes in the world. We do not know the big picture but if we walk listening to the still small voice of the spirit, God can bring his plans in to being. Christ is now bringing the light of his love to the people of Kosovo. What a wonderful joy and a privilege it is when we see God using us to bring about his purposes in this world and in the lives of those around us. What better reward than seeing souls saved for the Kingdom.

Psalm 138:8 The Lord will fulfil, His purpose for me.

Proverbs 19: 21 Many are the plans in a man's heart, but it is the Lord's purpose that prevails.

Chapter 19

Behold children are a heritage from the Lord

Behold, children are a heritage from the Lord, the fruit of the womb is a reward. Like arrows in the hand of a warrior, so are the children of one's youth. Happy is the man who has his quiver full of them. Psalm 127: 3-5

Bringing up children is never an easy task, every parent faces difficulties to a lesser or greater degree during their lifetime. I say lifetime, as bringing up children is a lifetime commitment, it doesn't end when they get to eighteen, the problems are just different. I praise God for my three dear children daily, each one as different as chalk and cheese, but each one loved as much as the other. Each one coming with a new set of challenges joys and sorrows.

Psalm 5:5 A father to the fatherless, a defender of widows, is God in His holy dwelling

My first two children didn't have the best start in life as their father left us when they were very small and for many years we were a one-parent family. Not that I am saying here that one parent families can't very successfully bring up their children, but it is harder and brings different challenges. In this modern day and age it is more acceptable for one-parent families and I would agree that a happy home with one parent is far better than a miserable life with two. However it was God's plan for us to be a family, father and mother working together to raise their sons and daughters, and I believe having experienced both sides of the coin, that God's way is the best way. The best for the children and for the parents. I praise

God daily that he provided for me a new father for my two children, but I know that if He hadn't, He would have given me the strengths needed and stood with me in bringing up my children.

Honour your father and mother that it may go well with you and that you may enjoy long life on the earth. Fathers, do not exasperate your children, instead, bring them up in the training and instruction of the Lord. Ephesians 6: 1-4

As parents it is very important to work together, supporting each other in decision-making and discipline, not taking sides with the children against each other but standing firm, even when you may think differently. We can discuss our differences in private. It is important to lead by example, showing love and respect, always speaking well about each other. At those times when disagreements come as they do in every marriage hold it and keep it for private time. Our children will learn how to behave and how to love from our examples. When my much loved Dad passed away and I was asked to say a few words about his life at the funeral, of all the things he did and achieved during his lifetime, it was the fact that he loved us all unconditionally, was always there when we needed him, and his love of mum, which was the greatest gift of all. The greatest example and a wonderful legacy. We were so blessed to have him as our father and although life is empty without him it is better because of him. I pray my children can say the same of me.

Train a child in the way he should go, and when he is old he will not turn from it.   Proverbs 2:6

During their teenage years Lorna and Peter gave us many occasions to put those principles into practice. Peter used to fight and argue with Roger about everything and anything pushing every boundary he could. I used to dread Peter coming home from college as I new our peace was going to be disrupted. The arguments affected the whole home and caused an unpleasant atmosphere. If I tried to bring peace to the argument it only got worse, so I could only pray and wait on the Lord. Bit by bit with the help of the Holy Spirit Roger begun not responding to the attacks from Peter, we would just let him fire off and stay quiet. We would give advice when asked, be there and just love him. Peter would behave in every way possible to make us despair of him. But no, we had decided not to believe all the stories we heard of how he did this or did that we decided to believe what we knew the Lord thought of him. A precious child bought and purchased by the blood of Christ. We tried in all circumstances to believe only the best. As parents if we can't believe the best of our children who can? Our Heavenly Father believes only the best of us and look at the mess we make of it at times.

Slowly and gradually the atmosphere begun to change, love took authority of the situation.

Isaiah 49: 25 I will contend with those who contend with you and your children I will save.

Although both Peter and Lorna had given their lives to the Lord the attractions of the world and the encouragement of their peers led them astray. Neither of them could understand why we wouldn't allow them to sleep with their boyfriends or girlfriends and why we wouldn't entertain this behaviour at home. This became to be one of the hardest principles to put into practice, for we knew that by keeping our stand and not allowing it within the home they were moving further and further away from us until they both left home to do what they wanted. No parent wants their child to leave because of disagreement but we knew that it would be wrong of us to not stand up for what we believed. To do anything else would be a denial of all we believed as Christians. For a while we lost them, for which I am sad, but praise God that today our relationship is restored and although they have not yet come to the point where they agree with us on this point, they understand our standing up for what we believe. Through this season and through others that have happened over the years when faced with seeing our children take the wrong road, or make the wrong decision we have found it better not to condemn or condone their behaviour but just to be there for them. Praying for them and loving them unconditionally as our Father in Heaven does us. For otherwise you can build a wall between you, cause a breakdown in your relationship and consequently destroy any chance of them having a relationship with their Heavenly Father. Always the door is open; always our love is there waiting, like in the story of the prodigal son, and how happy we will be when they come home to Christ.

Isaiah 59: 1 Surely the arm of the Lord is not too short to save; nor his hear too dull to hear.

There were times with Lorna when I became fearful for her by the way she was living. One night I had a dream. She was a little girl about 5years old and she had let go of my hand and was walking alone on the other side of the street. Lost and bewildered she begun to try and cross the road which was very busy. I cried out to her but couldn't reach her and I began to panic. At this point in my dream I awoke in tears. It was then the Lord showed me that although I was unable to change the situation and help Lorna, He was able, He was there taking care of her. She was in the best hands. This gave me a wonderful peace and from then onwards when faced with worrying circumstances I was able to pray and give it to the Lord knowing that He would look after my children.

Over the years we have seen their eyes being opened to the truth of the Gospel, they belong to the Lord, they are in His hands and we are fully confident that God will fulfil all the promises he has made to us for our children and our children's, children.

Isaiah 60:4-5 Lift up your eyes and look about you; All assemble and come to you; your sons come from afar, and your daughters are carried on the arm. Then; you will look and be radiant, your heart will throb and swell with joy.

Chapter 20

God works all things together for good

1 Samuel 1:27 I prayed for this child and the Lord granted me what I asked of him. So now I give him to the Lord.

Our youngest son, was born before Roger and I were married. When I first discovered I was pregnant, I was overjoyed but also rather afraid of our future and what others would think because of the circumstances. I prayed that the Lord would give me a healthy child and that Roger and I would be able to be married and that our lives would be blessed. In return I promised that I would bring him up in the faith and give him solely to the Lord. This I have done. Today Matthew is a strong Christian young man, serving the Lord. He has blessed our lives more than we can imagine. We know the Lord has a great plan and purpose for his future and we are honoured to be his parents.

Romans 8:28 All things God works for the good of those who love Him. Never think a situation is too bad, or that you've totally blown it. The Lord can turn those circumstances around and use them for his glory. He can make our greatest failure our greatest blessing.

1 Samuel 3:19,20 The Lord was with Samuel as he grew up and he let none of his words fall to the ground. And all Israel from Dan to Beersheba recognised that Samuel was attested as a prophet of the Lord.

As Matthew walks with the Lord he stands out to many people, young and old, as someone different, someone special. He enjoys life to the full, loves music, loves his friends, loves fun and gives 100% in all he does. He is always ready to help and has words of wisdom that surpass his years. He has always been such a great encouragement to me, and none more so than when Roger nearly lost his sight in 2007. Whilst Roger was in hospital and I waited at home for news of his operation I felt very anxious and I remember Matthew coming to sit with me and he said, "Don't worry Mum Jesus is in the boat". Just a few simple words but they were just what I needed to hear. To be reminded that Jesus was with us and to stay in faith, all would be well.

In this age where young people look to alcohol and drugs to give them a good time Matthew has no need of these, he finds his good time in life. Life with a capital L, for it is lived with Christ. Even when he was at University and challenged by his peers to join them in their drinking and smoking he was able to stand back and say no that's not for me. There is a better way. By standing firm in what he believes he is a shining star in a world of darkness. A great example. Matthew is often asked how is it that you find favour in so many things you do, and we truly believe that it is because of his faithfulness and commitment to the Lord. He is at the beginning of his journey but I know that the Lord is with him every step of the way, guiding, teaching, strengthening and equipping him for everything that comes across his path. And if he should wander from that path I know the Lord will lead him gently back. He has promised.

Chapter 21

Faithful One

Luke 2: 29,30 Sovereign Lord, as you have promised, you now dismiss your servant in peace. For my eyes have seen your Salvation.

One of my hearts cries has been for my parents to come to the knowledge of Jesus as their Lord and Saviour and for them to live with the hope of glory in their hearts. Over the years we have had many interesting discussions and arguments about our faith. I am standing on the scripture God gave us when we started our ministry, Autumn Harvest to the elderly. Psalm 91:16 With long life will I satisfy them and show them my salvation.

My father had been bought up attending church and singing in the church choir as a boy, even singing in St. Paul's Cathedral in London. However over the years he lost the desire to go to church and during the second world war he also lost his faith in God. Seeing so many of his friends and family killed in action and during the blitz, he could not believe there was a God.

When Dad was eighty three he needed heart surgery, following which he suffered cardiac arrest and remained in a coma for several weeks. It was our constant prayer during this time for Dad to meet with Jesus and have the assurance of his place in Heaven. Even though he was in a coma we prayed that the Lord would minister to him. During this time God gave me a scripture from the book of Luke 2: 25-32. When the baby Jesus was presented in the Temple there was an old man named Simeon waiting for a sign of the salvation of Israel. It had been revealed to him by the Holy Spirit that he would not die before he had seen the Christ. When Jesus parents brought Jesus in, Simeon took him in his arms and praised God saying, "Sovereign Lord, as you have promised you now dismiss your servant in peace. For my eyes have seen your salvation, which you have prepared in the sight of all people, a light for revelation to the gentiles and for glory to your people Israel." Simeon had seen the Christ and could then die in peace. I felt the Holy Spirit speak to me through this scripture giving me assurance that Dad would not die until he had met Jesus. Eventually Dad came out of the coma but had suffered major brain damage which had left him with no consciousness of who we were or what was going on. However we continued to pray with him, then one day when we were visiting he opened his eyes and said he saw Jesus standing at the end of his bed. In that moment I believe that Jesus ministered to him and when a few days later he passed away I knew Dad was with the Lord. The scripture had been fulfilled and he did not die before he had seen Christ. Praise God.

Though a situation may seem hopeless, nothing is too difficult for God and hard as it might be, we need to stay in faith praying and believing that what God says He will do.

Today I pray for Mum. For her salvation and for Gods wonderful peace to be with her. I trust in my God fully, knowing that He is faithful and that His mercies are new every morning.

Faithful One - Brian Doerksen

Faithful One so unchanging,
Ageless One your my rock of peace.
Lord of all I depend on you,
I call out to you, again and again.
You are my rock in times of trouble,
You lift me up when I fall down.
All through the storm Your love is the anchor,
my hope is in You alone.

Chapter 22

Persevere

Hebrews 12:1 Let us throw off every thing that hinders and the sin that so easily entangles, and let us run with perseverance the race marked out for us. Let us fix our eyes on Jesus, the author and perfector of our faith who for the joy set before Him endured the cross, scorning its shame and sat down at the right hand of the throne of God.

There are times in life when we are challenged. Testing times come and we take our eyes of Jesus and the race marked out for us. The devil is prowling around waiting for someone to devour, he wants to stop us and the plans and purposes God has for us. It is so easy to get off course when we take our eyes off the author and perfector of our faith. Jesus didn't give up when the going got tough. When faced with the cross, when His heart was troubled beyond measure. He said in John 12:27 Now my heart is troubled, and what shall I say? Father save me from this hour? No it was for this very reason I came to this hour. He knew the race set before Him and He knew He had to complete it. We need to remember what the Lord has done for us, get back into that place of prayer, turn our eyes back on Jesus, go back to the well and drink from the living water. Not turn to the left or to the right but look straight ahead. Take our eyes off our problems and run the race marked out for us with perseverance. . We need to remember whatever we are going through we are coming through. In all things we have the victory in Christ Jesus. He is our strength and our shield. We are more than conquerors, no weapon formed against us will prosper, the devil will not knock us off the race marked out for us.

Roger and I ministered in the old age homes for many years, it was a wonderful privilege to take Jesus to those dear ones, we saw lives changed and people filled with a hope for tomorrow as they have experienced a touch of God's love. However, if I am honest sometimes I became frustrated and wanted more. I hadn't seen what God had been doing only what I thought He hadn't done. There seemed to be so many old folks homes in Folkestone so many people who needed to be touched with the love of God. The harvest is so great but the labourers are few. I became weary and felt that we were getting nowhere. Sometimes I felt that the anointing had gone, that may be it was the end of our season leading Autumn Harvest, that it was time to hand it over to someone else. May be you feel this way about your life. Feel like giving up. Or may be you are struggling to do what the Lord is calling you to do. The Lord calls us to persevere. Hebrews 10: 16 You need to persevere so that when you have done the will of God, you will receive what He has promised. We need to remember what God has promised. Remember what God has done for you, how far you have come. The Lord tells us to press on. Philippians 3:14 Press on toward the goal to win the prize for which God has called us heavenwards in Christ Jesus.

We must persevere not just in deeds but press forward in prayer, for it is in the place of prayer our ministry takes flight. Where God's love and purpose for His people is born inside us, where we receive the gifting and the anointing to do all God would have us do. I remember when the Lord first asked us to minister to the old folks my flesh cried, no not old people, grumpy, smelly, boring old people; I am called to children's ministry. But as I prayed the Lord showed me them as He sees them, He showed me His love for them, showed me that He hadn't forgotten them, that they have a wonderful hope and future in Him. When I saw this I could do nothing except say, yes, yes send me I will go. He places His love in our hearts and as we pray His heart becomes our heart, His desires become our desires. We need to remember this when the devil would try to knock us of course, remember your first love, turn our eyes back on Jesus and the promise and prize set before us.

When those trials come against us whatever they may be, sickness, family problems, financial difficulties and we feel we cannot continue. Remember God say's in James 1:12 Blessed is the man who perseveres under trial because when he has stood the test, he will receive the crown of life that God has promised to those who love Him.

Don't give up, press on.

Galatians 6:9 Let us not grow weary in doing good for at the proper time we will reap a harvest if we do not give up. The fields are ripe for harvest and harvest time is now. There are so many who need to hear the good news of the gospel.

Whatever God has called or is calling you to do, do it to the best of your ability. He will strengthen you and uphold you as you serve Him. Be steadfast and do not take your eyes off the master.

Persevere run the race marked out for you!!

Epilogue

I am so thankful to God for all He has done in my life, how He took a broken young woman and changed her to the person I am today. None of us know what tomorrow may bring, but one thing I do know is that Jesus will be with me through it all and that one day I will see Him face to face. I have a living hope for today and bright hope for tomorrow.

In conclusion I leave you the words of this wonderful song by Fanny Crosby and I pray that my words have encouraged you in your walk with Jesus. What He has done for me, He wants to and can do for you. May God bless you.

All the way my Saviour leads me - Fanny J Crosby

All the way my Saviour leads me
What have I to ask beside
Can I doubt His tender mercy
Who through life has been my guide
Heavenly peace, divinest comfort
Here by faith in Him to dwell
For I know what'er befall me
Jesus doeth all things well.

All the way my Saviour leads me
Cheers each winding path I tread
He gives me grace for every trial
Feeds me with the living bread
And though my weary steps may falter
And my soul athirst may be
Gushing from the rock before me
Lo a spring of joy I see

And all the way my Saviour leads me
Oh the fullness of His love
Perfect rest to me is promised
In my Father's house above
And when my spirit clothed immortal
Wings its flight to realms of day
This my song through endless ages
Jesus led me all the way.

Amen.